C000045554

# A CULINARY JOURNEY

Exploring destinations and discovering different cultures and traditions is at the heart of every Viking journey. And of course food – not only the recipes prepared by our onboard chefs, but also local cuisine in all the fascinating places our ships visit – is an essential part of the overall Viking experience.

We hope this book helps you to recreate the flavors of your travels back home in your own kitchen, and inspires you to continue exploring the world.

# NORTHERN
# EUROPE

Historically, the Romans had a huge influence on the
development of northern Europe's cuisine, and preferred
boiling and stewing their meat over roasting since smoke
and fat were reserved for the Gods. During the Middle Ages
and Renaissance, meat became the central part of the meal.
European cuisine was further developed in the royal and
noble courts, and in the 18th and 19th centuries 'cuisine
classique' – a mix of aristocratic and French bourgeois
cuisine – became the culinary standard in Europe. There is an
emphasis on comforting soups and stews, and in countries
like Austria, The Netherlands and Germany, smoking, curing,
pickling and salting of foods is common. Much of the region,
particularly Romania, is also involved in wine production.

# THE
# NETHERLANDS

Splendid windmill-studded tulip fields,
colorful Amsterdam and a rich culture
make The Netherlands an idyllic
destination for sightseeing. Simple and
straightforward, Dutch cuisine has been
shaped by fishing and farming, with lots
of seafood, vegetables, breads
and cheeses on offer.

# BITTERBALLEN

## Serves 4–6

small onion, finely
chopped

¾ oz (50g) butter

tbsp all purpose
(plain) flour

0 fl oz (300ml) beef
stock or leftover gravy

tbsp fresh parsley,
chopped

4 oz (400g) cooked
beef, shredded

alt and pepper

utmeg, grated

egetable oil, for frying

oz (55g) all purpose
(plain) flour

eggs, beaten

oz (85g) breadcrumbs

**1** To make the roux (a mixture of butter and flour used to thicken sauces), fry the onion in the butter until soft and translucent, then stir in the flour. Continue to cook until the mixture is pale and bubbling, then slowly whisk in the beef stock to make a very thick sauce.

**2** Stir in the parsley and the cooked beef and season with the salt and pepper. Add a grating of nutmeg, then set aside to cool.

**3** To make the bitterballen, take a tablespoon of the cold beef mixture and, with floured hands, quickly roll it into a ball, then coat with the beaten egg, and then finally with the breadcrumbs. Heat the oil until shimmering hot, then fry in batches until golden brown. Serve with mustard.

# CREAMY CHEESE SOUP

**Serves 4**

4 tbsp oil
1 tbsp butter
1 large white onion
2-3 slices smoked
  streaky bacon,
  chopped
1 cauliflower, broken
  into florets
6 oz (170g) potatoes,
  peeled and chopped
4 large carrots, peeled
  and chopped
1 tbsp fresh thyme
1 pint (475ml) chicken
  stock
5 oz (140g) Gouda
  cheese, grated
4 tbsp heavy (double)
  cream
Salt and pepper, to taste

FOR THE CARAMELIZED
WALNUTS:
2 ½ oz (70g) walnuts,
  roasted
1 oz (30g) sugar
1 tbsp water

**1** Add the oil and butter to a heavy frying pan and fry the onion and bacon until sizzling. Add in the cauliflower, potatoes and carrots and continue to cook on a low heat until softened.
**2** Add in the fresh thyme, then stir in the chicken stock. Bring to a boil, then simmer until all the vegetables are tender. Add the cheese and cream, then blend with a stick blender until very smooth. Season to taste.
**3** To make the caramelized walnuts, heat the sugar and water until it forms a thick syrup, then coat the walnuts with the syrup and allow to cool on a non-stick baking sheet.

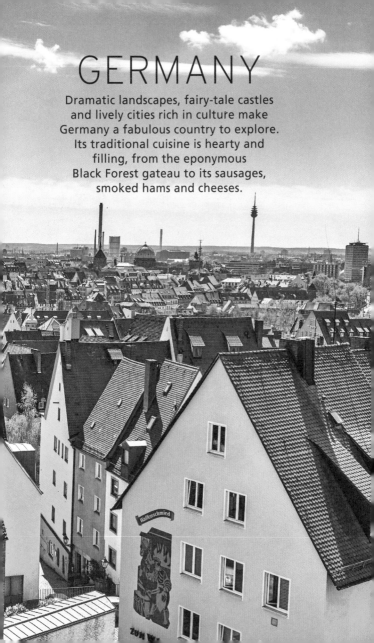

# GERMANY

Dramatic landscapes, fairy-tale castles
and lively cities rich in culture make
Germany a fabulous country to explore.
Its traditional cuisine is hearty and
filling, from the eponymous
Black Forest gateau to its sausages,
smoked hams and cheeses.

# SPÄTZLE

**Serves 4**

1.1 lb (500g) all purpose
 (plain) flour
Large pinch salt
Grated nutmeg
 (optional)
4 large eggs, beaten
10 fl oz (300ml) milk
2 tsp salt

**1** It is possible to make spätzle by hand, but you'll find it much easier to use a stand mixer. Place the flour and salt into the bowl and grate in a little nutmeg.

**2** Make a well in the center and add in the beaten egg. Mix with the dough hook attachment for 15 to 20 minutes or until holes start to appear in the dough.

**3** Bring a large pan of water to the boil and add 2 tsp salt. With a flexible spatula, press the dough through the holes of a colander over the water to make the spätzle.

**4** As the noodles float to the top (within three to five minutes), remove with a slotted spoon and place in a bowl of iced water.

**5** When all the spätzle are cooked, drain and drizzle with a little oil to prevent them sticking together. To serve, warm through with a little melted butter and chopped, fresh parsley.

# BLACK FOREST GATEAU

**Serves 6–8**

6 oz (170g) butter, at
room temperature

6 oz (170g) superfine
(caster) sugar

6 large eggs, whisked

5 oz (140g) all purpose
(plain) flour

2 tsp baking powder

2 tbsp cocoa powder

1 ½ lb (680g) black
cherries in kirsch syrup

1.6 pints (750ml) heavy
(double) cream

7 oz (200g) bar of dark
chocolate

**1** To make the cakes, preheat the oven to
350°F (180°C) and grease and line two large
(9 inch/23cm) springform cake tins.

**2** Beat the butter and sugar together until pale
and creamy, then slowly add about half the eggs.

**3** Sift together the flour, baking powder and
cocoa and add about half to the butter and sugar
mixture, then add the remaining eggs and finally
the remaining flour mixture.

**4** Split the mixture evenly between the two
cake tins and level the tops. Bake for about 30
minutes or until the cakes are springy to the
touch. Set aside to cool.

**5** Drain the cherries, reserving the liquid. Set 12
aside and chop the rest into small pieces.

**6** Halve each of the cooled cakes horizontally.
Whip the cream until stiff peaks start to form.

**7** To assemble, start with one of the cake halves.
Drizzle generously with kirsch syrup, then
spread over a thick layer of whipped cream.
Scatter over a third of the chopped cherries.
Repeat again with the next two layers. For the
final layer, drizzle with kirsch syrup, then cover
the cake with the remaining cream.

**8** For the chocolate shards, brace the chocolate
against you, flat side up, and carefully bring the
blade of a sharp knife towards you, shaving the
chocolate into curls and shards. Shower the top
and sides of the cake with the chocolate shards.
Finally, top with the remaining whole cherries.

# AUSTRIA

From its magnificent capital, Vienna, the
Danube River and the music of Mozart,
Strauss, Schubert and Haydn, Austria is
utterly enchanting. Game is a traditional
element of Austrian cuisine, along
with seasonal vegetables and fruits like
pumpkin. Wiener Schnitzel, exquisite
pastries and desserts are all highlights.

# WIENER SCHNITZEL

**Serves 4**

4 veal escalopes, approx
4 ½ oz (125g) per
person

4 ½ oz (125g) all
purpose (plain) flour

Salt and pepper

2 eggs, beaten

8 oz (225g) breadcrumbs

9 oz (255g) butter

1 lb (450g) potatoes,
cooked, peeled and
sliced

2 oz (55g) butter

Small bunch fresh
parsley

1 lemon

**1** Place the veal escalopes on a board and gently tap with a rolling pin until thin and even. Breadcrumb the veal escalopes by preparing three plates: one with the flour, seasoned generously, one with the beaten eggs and one with the breadcrumbs. Dip the escalopes first in the flour, brushing off the excess, then in the egg wash and then into the breadcrumbs, pressing them firmly onto the meat.

**2** Heat the butter in a heavy based pan and skim off any residue. Deep fry the escalopes in the butter, basting frequently, until golden brown, then drain on kitchen towel. Keep warm.

**3** Serve the escalopes with boiled potatoes (boiled in water with butter) and garnish with chopped parsley and a lemon wedge.

 Discover more at *exploringmore.com/video/wienerschnitzel*

# SACHERTORTE

**Serves 8–10**

5 oz (140g) butter,
  softened
3 ½ oz (100g)
  confectioners' (icing)
  sugar, sieved
8 eggs, separated
5 oz (140g) bittersweet
  (dark) chocolate
2 ¾ oz (80g) all purpose
  (plain) flour
3 ½ oz (100g) sugar
2 tbsp apricot jam

**FOR THE GLAZE:**

8 oz (225g) bittersweet
  (dark) chocolate
2 tbsp butter

**1** Preheat oven to 375°F (190°C) and grease and line a 9 inch (23cm) cake tin. Cream together the butter and icing sugar, then mix in the egg yolks, one at a time, until very creamy.

**2** Melt the chocolate in a heatproof bowl placed over a saucepan of simmering water. Do not allow the bowl to touch the water. Gradually add the melted chocolate into the creamed mixture, then fold in the flour.

**3** In a separate bowl, beat the egg whites until they form soft peaks and then gradually fold in the sugar. Combine this mixture with the chocolate mixture.

**4** Pour the cake mixture into the prepared tin and bake for about 50 minutes to an hour until springy to the touch. Remove from the pan and cool on a wire rack. Heat the apricot jam and smooth over the entire torte, including the sides.

**5** For the glaze, melt the chocolate and butter together in a bain-marie until smooth and glossy. Pour over the cake, making sure it's completely covered, and allow to cool before serving.

 Discover more at *exploringmore.com/video/sachertorte*

# CZECH REPUBLIC

Located at the heart of Central Europe, this small nation boasts spectacular cultural treasures and a rich tapestry of natural wonders, such as the stunning cliffs along the River Elbe. Influenced by its surrounding countries, potato soup, roast pork and dumplings all feature heavily in its cuisine. Whilst bread is traditionally baked from rye and wheat.

# RYE BREAD

**Makes 2 loaves**

14 oz (400g) strong
  white bread flour
11 ½ oz (325g) rye flour
2 x ¼ oz (7g) packs of
  fast action dried yeast
1 tbsp salt
1 tbsp sugar
2 tsp caraway seeds
1 tbsp fennel seeds
3 tbsp lard (vegetable
  shortening)
1 pint (475ml) water

**1** In a large mixing bowl, combine the flours with the yeast, salt, sugar and seeds. Mix well.
**2** In a saucepan, gently heat the water and lard until the lard has melted. Slowly pour the hot liquid into the flour mixture, stirring all the time just until the dough comes together. You may not need to add all the liquid, but the dough should be quite sticky.
**3** Knead the dough for about 5 minutes, either in a food processor with a dough hook or by hand (although it is easier in a food processor as the dough benefits from being really moist). Cover with a clean cloth and allow to rise somewhere warm for about an hour.
**4** Punch the dough down, divide in two and shape into round loaves. Place on a non-stick baking sheet and allow to rise for a further 30 minutes. Preheat the oven to 375°F (190°C) and bake for 35 to 40 minutes until golden brown and hollow when tapped.

# CHEF MAREK'S CZECH DUCK

**Serves 4**

4 small to medium white
  onions, peeled
Olive oil
3 ½ oz (100g) butter,
  cubed
3.5 fl oz (100ml) apple
  cider vinegar
3.5 fl oz (100ml) good
  quality veal stock
1 vanilla bean
4 duck breasts, skin on
1 garlic clove, crushed
2 sprigs thyme
20-25 green, seedless
  grapes, peeled
Salt and pepper

**1** Preheat the oven to 350°F (175°C). Place the onions in a small, heavy based roasting tin or Dutch oven. Drizzle generously with olive oil and dot each onion with a small knob of butter. Cover with a lid or tightly with foil and bake for 40 minutes to an hour until completely soft.

**2** Meanwhile, make the cider vinegar reduction for the glazed grapes: add the vinegar to a pan, bring to the boil then allow to bubble and reduce down to about 1 fl oz (30ml).

**3** For the veal jus, pour the veal stock into a pan, split the vanilla bean, scrape out the seeds and add to the stock. Bring to the boil then reduce down, by about ¾ to a thick, shiny sauce.

**4** Heat a large, dry frying pan on the hob. Score the skin of the duck breasts in a criss-cross pattern and sprinkle with salt and pepper.

**5** Place the duck breast skin side down in the pan. Add the crushed whole garlic clove and the thyme and cook until the skin is golden.

**6** Turn the duck breast over, then add a couple of cubes of butter onto the duck and place in the oven for 8 minutes. Remove and leave to rest, basting with the cooking liquid.

**7** To assemble, add the grapes to the cider vinegar reduction, with some salt and pepper. Stir in a couple of cubes of butter. Cook for a couple of minutes then remove from the heat.

**8** To serve, top the mashed potato with the sliced duck and glazed grapes. Pour over the veal jus.

 Discover more at *exploringmore.com/video/duck*

# HUNGARY

Hungary has survived wars and
occupations and contributed much to
the arts and sciences; it is also home
to one of the most beautiful cities in
Europe, the capital Budapest. Hungarian
food is hearty and filling, and includes
goulash, stuffed peppers, cabbage
rolls and strudels.

# GOULASH

## Serves 4–6

2 tbsp oil

1 large onion, finely chopped

2 lb (900g) lean stewing steak

3 carrots, chopped

3 celery stalks, chopped

2 cloves garlic, sliced

1 green bell pepper, deseeded and chopped

2 large tomatoes, skinned and chopped

3 pints (1.4l) beef stock

2 tsp paprika

1 lemon

Salt and pepper

3 large white potatoes, peeled and chopped

Sour cream

**1** In a large pot, heat the oil, then fry the onion for about five minutes until softened. Add the beef and fry, stirring constantly, until completely browned (add a little more oil if necessary).

**2** Add the carrots, celery, garlic and chopped pepper, then fry for a further five minutes.

**3** Stir in the tomato, stock and paprika. Season generously with salt and pepper and add a good squeeze of lemon juice. Turn the heat up and bring to a boil, then lower the heat, cover and simmer for about 1 hour and 30 minutes, until the meat is completely tender. Add the potatoes about 20 minutes before the end of the cooking time. Serve in bowls and garnish with a large spoonful of sour cream.

 Discover more at *exploringmore.com/video/goulash*

# CHICKEN PÖRKÖLT

**Serves 4**

4 chicken breasts, cubed,
  or 1 whole chicken, cut
  into pieces
3 tbsp olive oil
1 onion, chopped
1 green bell pepper,
  deseeded and chopped
3 cloves garlic, sliced
3 tbsp paprika
1 pinch dried chili
  flakes
14 oz (400g) tinned
  chopped tomatoes in
  their juice
1 pint (475ml) chicken
  stock
2 bay leaves
Salt and pepper

**1** In a heavy based casserole dish, heat the oil, then fry the onion and green pepper for about five minutes until softened. Add the garlic, paprika and chili flakes, and stir well.

**2** Pour in the chopped tomatoes and stock. Season generously with salt and pepper, add the bay leaves, then stir in the meat. Turn the heat up and bring to a boil, then lower the heat, cover and simmer for about an hour, until the meat is completely tender.

**3** Serve immediately with pasta or gnocchi.

# PORTUGAL

In its coastal cities, including Porto and Lisbon, fresh seafood reigns supreme, in particular *bacalhau* (salted cod stews) and sardines. In the lush Douro Valley, renowned for its wine, popular dishes include roasted goat and wild boar stew. Traditional breads are also fantastic.

# BACALHAU À BRÁS

**Serves 4**

1 lb (450g) dried
  salted cod
1 lb (450g) waxy
  potatoes
Olive oil
1 large white onion,
  halved, then thinly
  sliced
2 bay leaves
4 cloves garlic, crushed
2 tbsp fresh parsley,
  chopped
4 large eggs
1 oz (30g) black olives,
  pitted

TO GARNISH:
Dash of Tabasco
Lemon wedges

**1** Cover the dried cod in cold water and allow to soak for approximately 48 hours, changing the water frequently.

**2** Place the cod in a large pot and cover with water again. Boil for about 15 minutes, then drain. Allow to cool, then flake and set aside.

**3** Peel the potatoes and cut into matchsticks. Add 1 to 2 tablespoons of olive oil to a non-stick pan and fry the potatoes in batches. Keep the cooked matchsticks warm in a low oven.

**4** Add a further tablespoon of olive oil to the pan and add the bay leaves. Cook for two to three minutes, then add the garlic and onions to the pan. Sauté until translucent. Discard the bay leaves, and then add in the parsley and the flaked cod.

**5** Mix the eggs with a fork, then add to the pan. Keep stirring until the eggs are scrambled. Combine the fries with the cod mixture, then stir in the olives. Season to taste and finish with a dash of Tabasco. Garnish with lemon wedges.

 Discover more at *exploringmore.com/video/bacalhau*

# PASTÉIS DE NATA

**Makes roughly 12**

8 ½ fl oz (250ml) milk
1 lemon, zest only
1 cinnamon stick
3 ½ oz (100g) superfine
   (caster) sugar
2 tbsp all purpose
   (plain) flour
2 ½ fl oz (75ml) water
3 large eggs, yolks only
11 ¼ oz (320g) all-butter
   puff pastry

**1** Preheat the oven to 475°F (245°C). Gently heat the milk with two to three strips of lemon zest and the cinnamon stick to a simmer, then remove the lemon and cinnamon.

**2** Mix the flour with a little of the milk to form a smooth paste, then stir in the rest of the milk. Return to the heat, whisking constantly for a few minutes until thick.

**3** Place the sugar and water in a saucepan, stirring until the sugar has dissolved. Bring to a boil and allow to boil for three minutes, then whisk into the milk mixture.

**4** Place the egg yolks in a bowl and slowly add the milk mixture, whisking constantly. Transfer to a jug and allow to cool slightly.

**5** Lightly butter all the holes in a 12-hole muffin tin. Roll the pastry out into a rough rectangle, then roll each rectangle up from the bottom to the top. Cut each roll into 12 discs. Place one disc flat into the base of each muffin hole, then, with wet thumbs, gently press out until the pastry comes about half way up each hole.

**6** Pour the custard into the pastry cases, then bake for about 15 minutes, until set and caramelized. Sprinkle with sugar and cinnamon, then serve while still warm.

# FRANCE

As you might expect, cheese and wine
play a major part in all French cuisine,
but each region has its own specialty.
In Normandy dishes made with seafood
and apples are abundant; Provence
and the Côte d'Azur are renowned for
fresh vegetables, fruits and herbs; and
in Burgundy, specialties include pike,
perch, snails, game, redcurrants
and blackcurrants.

# BOEUF BOURGUIGNON

**Serves 4**

Olive oil

3 ½ oz (100g) bacon
  lardons

1 large white onion,
  sliced

2 tbsp all purpose
  (plain) flour

Salt and pepper

1.3 lb (590g) lean
  stewing steak

1 bottle (750ml)
  Burgundy or other
  good red wine

1 garlic clove, crushed

1 bouquet garni

6 oz (170g) button
  mushrooms

6 oz (170g) whole baby
  onions

**1** Preheat the oven to 325°F (160°C). Heat two tablespoons of olive oil in a heavy casserole dish and fry the bacon lardons until golden brown. Remove from the pan and reserve. Repeat with the sliced onion, frying until soft.

**2** Mix the flour together with a generous amount of salt and pepper and toss the steak well in the seasoned flour. Shake off the excess, then fry the steak in batches until well browned, adding more oil if needed.

**3** Deglaze the pan with a glassful of red wine. Allow the liquid to bubble and scrape all the caramelized bits from the bottom of the pan. Return the bacon, onions and beef to the pan with the garlic and bouquet garni. Pour in the rest of the red wine. If the meat isn't completely covered, add a little beef stock or water.

**4** Put on a lid and place the casserole in the oven. Cook for about 2 ½ hours.

**5** About 30 minutes before the end of the cooking time, fry the baby onions and mushrooms until golden and add to the beef. Remove the bouquet garni before serving.

# TARTE TATIN

**Serves 6**

3 ½ oz (100g) superfine
  (caster) sugar
2 oz (55g) butter
6 dessert apples
2 tbsp butter
11.2 oz (320g) all-butter
  puff pastry

**1** Preheat the oven to 350°F (175°C). Heat the sugar and butter over a medium heat until it turns a deep golden brown. Don't allow the caramel to burn.

**2** Peel and halve the apples, scooping out the seeds with a spoon. Place all the apples in the caramel and cook, moving them around in the caramel, for about 10 minutes. Next, in a 9 inch (23cm) diameter oven proof dish or pan, arrange the apple halves, rounded side down. Fill in any gaps with cut apples and dot with small pieces of butter.

**3** Roll the pastry out into a circle, slightly larger than the pan and about 0.2 inch (5mm) thick. Place the disc of pastry over the caramelized apples, tucking the edges in all around the dish. Brush with melted butter.

**4** Bake for around 30 to 40 minutes, or until the pastry is golden brown and the caramel is starting to ooze from the tart. Leave to cool for an hour before serving.

# ROMANIA

Packed with cultural highlights,
Romania's cuisine is also a treasure
waiting to be discovered. With an
emphasis on hearty, homemade food,
many of the dishes are influenced by
neighboring countires. Expect lots of
soup, cabbage stews and minced meat.

# MITITEI

**Makes around 20**

1 lb (450g) ground
  (minced) beef
1 lb (450g) lean ground
  (minced) pork
2 tsp baking soda
  (bicarbonate of soda)
2 tbsp water
2 garlic cloves, crushed
2 tsp dried thyme
2 tsp caraway seeds
½ tsp ground allspice
1 tsp ground coriander
½ tsp hot paprika
2 tsp salt
1 tsp freshly ground
  black pepper

1 Place the beef and pork in a large bowl. Dissolve the baking soda in the water and add into the meat along with the garlic and all the spices and seasoning.

2 Using either a food mixer or clean hands, knead the mixture together thoroughly for at least five minutes, then transfer the mixture to a clean bowl, cover and refrigerate for a few hours or, ideally, overnight.

3 Keep a bowl of clean water near and with wet hands, form the meat into small sausages, around 4 inches (10cm) in length.

4 To cook, either grill the mititei on a barbecue, or grill for 10 to 12 minutes until they are cooked through. Serve with mustard, French fries, and a cold beer.

**First published in Germany in 2018 by Viking**

**Copyright © Viking**

ISBN 978-1-909968-34-9

Book design by The Chelsea Magazine Company Limited

Photography: James Murphy
Additional images: AWL Images, Getty Images, iStock, StockFood
Recipe testing: Rebecca Wiggins

Printed and bound in Germany by Mohn Media

**vikingcruises.com**